Tales from Northern Arizona
Bob's Blogs, Essays, and Short Stories

By Robert Darrol Shanks Jr., PhD

Copyright © 2024 Robert Darrol Shanks Jr. PhD

Cover Photo by Bob Shanks was taken at the Sharlot Hall Museum in Prescott, Arizona.

Published by: Writers Publishing House
Printed in the United States

ISBN: 978-1-64873-495-3

All rights reserved. No part of this book may be reproduced in any manner whatsoever without written permission from the author except in the case of brief quotations embodied in critical articles and reviews.

To the Reader

Tales from Northern Arizona is a series of short stories, essays, and (for those familiar with computers) blogs. The word "blog" is and remains somewhat of a mystery to me, it applies only to articles and stories written using a word program based on a computer system.

Growing up in Nebraska in a different and simpler time of history in America, I learned to read at an early age, as my mother told the story, I almost caused my dad to crash his car as his small three-year-old blond headed son Bobby looked out the car window and read a sign printed on the side of a filling station building and then said "Ice" to his parents. Since I was the only child at the time my mother and father had not expected this little boy riding in the back seat of a car to read a sign and then speak so clearly about what he read since he was not even in school yet!

After graduating from high school in Grand Island, Nebraska I enlisted in the United States Air Force (USAF).

I wanted to attend college and my high school counselor recommended I go to college as well. However, growing up in a family of six, my father, Robert D. Shanks Sr., worked on the Union Pacific Railroad and my mom was a stay-at-home homemaker. So, funds were scarce for attending college after high school. Jobs were not plentiful in Nebraska at that time since the state was primarily based on agriculture and farming. The military offered some travel, adventure, education, and training so I enlisted in the Air Force just after my 18th birthday and graduation from high school.

This author's first two books are Christian based, "A Father's Stories for His Children" and "An Awakening at Nain", all based on the Bible and scripture. This book is made up of short essays and writings based on growing up in Nebraska and serving in the United States Air Force and Air National Guard. After my four years serving in the Air Force, I attended college in Nebraska using the G.I. Bill obtaining my Bachelor's, Master's, and Doctor of Philosophy degrees in education from the University of Nebraska colleges located in Kearney and Lincoln, Nebraska. I stayed in the military by serving in the

Nebraska Air National Guard utilizing the guard's educational assistance programs for those pursuing a higher education.

I was also a teacher, teaching seventh, eighth and ninth grade at R.J. Barr Junior High in Grand Island, Nebraska. I taught English, journalism and special education. I also later served as a public-school administrator in Nebraska and later in Arizona.

I can't emphasize enough how important my walk in Christianity has been to me and my family. Our love for Jesus Christ, our trust in Him and all that He has done for humanity is amazing. Always take whatever issues that life has thrown at you to our Lord and Savior in prayer. A quote from the Bible that has always been close to my heart is found in Philippians 4:6-7:

"Do not be anxious about anything, but in every situation, by prayer and petition, with thanksgiving, present your request to God. And the peace of God, which transcends all understanding will guard your hearts and your minds in Christ Jesus."

Acknowledgements

This book is a small collection of short stories and essays, *"Tales from Northern Arizona"*, has been an adventure in getting my crazy imagination and fascination with literature and short stories on to paper. I could not have done this without the backing of my wife and soul mate **Cindi LaSalle-Shanks**. She has always stood by me in thick and thin in my moments of frustration and feelings of inadequacy to even attempt this little book. Her encouragement in my life is invaluable. She has been my proofreader and has suggested valuable changes and suggestions.

    Of course, my children are all so supportive, ***Krystal Lynne Klueckman, Kurenia Faye Barnes***, and ***Bradley Eric LaSalle***. Without such wonderful children, a father can lose sight of goals and objectives in life. This book is also for all my wonderful 13 grandchildren and for my seven-great grandchildren who are a constant delight and source of amazement. I owe a big thank you to them for helping me keep an innocence of attitude, the wonderment of discovery, the addition of new ideas and the maintenance of my positive view of life through Christianity.

Tales from Northern Arizona is dedicated to the memory of our four deceased children, **Robert Scott Shanks, Kandace Leigh Shanks-Tettleton, Steven Allan LaSalle**, and **Diana Lynn LaSalle-Hontz.**

Contents

To the Reader _____ *i*

Acknowledgements _____ *iv*

An Early American Colonist's Blacksmith Shop _____ *2*

One Way to Contribute to America's Greatness _____ *7*

Teaching Can Make a Difference _____ *10*

A Defining and Interesting Early Military Experience _ *23*

UFOs or UAPs Just What are They? _____ *26*

The Mystic and Wonder of Unidentifed Aerial Phenomenon (UAP) _____ *30*

Better Known in the Past as Unidentified Flying Objects (UFO)

Pentagon's Plan in Case Alien's Discovered _____ *34*

Problem Solving Steps - A Key to Success _____ *44*

The Art of Asking Good Questions _____ *52*

The Importance of Critical Thinking in Today's Topsey-Turvey Educational Systems _____ *55*

Write Something That Means Something Based on Verifiable Factual Information _____ *58*

The Five Levels of Situational Awareness _____ *61*

Finding the Right Level _____ *65*

Of Situational Awareness _____ *65*

Worldwide Terrorism is on the Rise _____ *69*

The CIA is Broken - Its Main Job: Protecting the U.S. from Threats _____ *72*

Military Noncombatant Evacuation Operation (NEO) _ *81*

Why is Christianity so Trivialized and Attacked? _____ *88*

Short Story Section _____ *92*

A Strange Old Hanger at the Airport! _____ *93*

The Old Tube Powered Radio Still Works _____ *97*

An Encounter at the Nightcrawlers Bar _____ *105*

A Strange Hearing Test _____ *111*

Is Interdimensional Travel a Real Possibility? _____ *115*

The Flying Mogollon Monster of Northern Arizona __ *123*

References _____ *127*

An Early American Colonist's
Blacksmith Shop

Alex wiped his brow with his grimy hand and paused for a moment to consider where he was and what he should do next. His Boston blacksmith workshop was smokey and smelled like gun powder. He was a long way from his home in the plains of the central part of the United States. It seemed strange to call the country the "United States" from its old name of "United Colonies" that was in widespread use at the time. The new name was eventually decreed by the Continental Congress in 1776. Alex often questioned himself as to why he was even here in Massachusetts. A revolutionary war seemed inevitable with the British. It seemed no matter what the Continental Congress did, the British were able control the progress and changes to their advantage. Alex and his little blacksmith shop could hardly keep up with customers coming into his local business.

The whole idea of a war with Britain was on the minds of many early American citizens beginning in 1760 to 1775 long before any blood was spilled at the battle of Lexington. After Great Britain's victory in the eight-year French and Indian war that ended in 1763 many colonists were emboldened to resist new British policies of taxation without representation, and fight for political rights, and individual freedoms.

Many early American patriots demanded independence and expanded individual rights. It seemed a confrontation with Great Britain was inevitable. Many felt the British policies unfair; citizens during that time had a sense of nationalism stimulated to demand separation of church and state, a right to representation in government and more control over their destinies and commercial power. As the year of 1775 proceeded these and many other governmental and business issues were surfacing in the American Colonies, it was indeed a tumultuous time for the American colonies under the rule of Great Britain.

And caught right in the middle of all of this political upheaval was Alex and his little blacksmith shop struggling to chart a business path of independence and self-regulation supporting his community and customer base. His business was thriving being used by both citizens and the British military.

Many Americans, but not all of them at that time, felt it was the countries destiny to spread out into the entire continent. The term "manifest destiny" would soon emerge and not everyone agreed about this general policy of imperialism. Tensions with Britain were increasing and led up to the infamous "Boston Tea Party" that allowed the British East India Company to sell tea from China in the colonies without paying taxes apart from those imposed by the Townshend Acts of that era. A group known as the "Sons of Liberty" strongly opposed the Townshend taxes as a violation of their rights resulting in the Boston Tea Party of 1773 destroying an entire shipment of tea sent by the East India Company. The group tossed it into Boston Harbor. A second ship of tea in Philadelphia was sent back to Britain without unloading it. War with Britain was looming on the horizon.

The resulting Revolutionary war turned out to be unlike any other war. The colonists' ideas and ideals of freedom helped to shape the emerging country's course of human events like no other war or event in history. The war has been described by historians as a major catalyst for Independence. The development of the  Declaration of Independence for individual inalienable rights for all citizens was indeed unique in history.

All students, no matter the school or level should study this period of U.S. history in detail and realize how fortunate they are to live in the United States of America.

This key American history should be a vital part of all public-school system's curriculum.

One Way to Contribute to America's Greatness

There are countless ways to contribute to America's greatness, but one way is for youth to consider serving in one of the branches of the U.S. military. For many of our youth, if post high school planning is not clear, the military can often offer many advantages for training and education. While military service may not be for everyone, it can be something just about every young person should consider.

President Kennedy's 1961 quote often comes to mind, *"Ask not what your country can to do for you - ask what you can do for your country."* Depending on family status, vocational or college interests, the military can offer countless advantages for training and education. For many it also can become a career.

For this writer, I wanted to attend college but not knowing what I really wanted to do, I joined the Air Force because of my keen interest in aviation and photography. After my four-year service as a photographer, I was able to attend college using the G.I. Bill, work part time as a photographer and with help from my family to graduate with a BA and gain my teaching certifications. I wanted to give back to our country so felt that my continued service in one of the reserve or guard components seemed like a good idea. Continued service in the reserve component also gave me help in getting my advanced degrees as well while serving in the Air National Guard and later in the U.S. Air Force Reserve. Often, various tours of duty needed assistance from the reserve component so since I was an educator, I could do short tours of duty in various military assignments as needed and could also take leaves of absence. Of course, not every job allows for this flexibility of military service but there is also a Federal Law stating employers must allow service in a reserve component. Youth need to be taught patriotism and service to this great country of ours. I fear we are in a slow decline primarily due to our poor educational systems.

Most civilizations only last about 250 years, Catholic writer Charles Pope outlined what he says are the eight stages of a civilization in a blog he wrote in 2016:

The question has to be can we slow this down? Can we as a country prevent it from happening? What stage are we really in now? It appears the sad truth of history is we cannot prevent it from happening.

The average age of the world's greatest civilizations is 200 years. Here's the sequence:

1. Bondage to spiritual faith
2. Spiritual faith to great courage
3. Great courage to liberty
4. Liberty to abundance
5. From abundance to selfishness
6. Selfishness to complacency
7. Complacency to apathy
8. Apathy to dependency
9. Dependency back into bondage

Teaching Can Make a Difference

Trey Gowdy, New York Times best-selling author, TV personality, former prosecutor, and congressman has a book entitled "Start, Stay or Leave". It is an excellent read about choosing a direction in life. He often tells young people who come to talk to him and want to change the world and make a difference to go into teaching.

As I read his book, I found myself thinking my entire career has been a teacher in some capacity teaching junior high school, teaching at colleges and universities and

I even taught hospitalized teenagers in a psychiatric hospital. One of my most memorable assignments was as a professor for the USAF Air War College teaching international military officers from over 42 countries. So, I have a host of memories to draw upon. However, I don't want anyone reading this to think I'm just blowing my horn and bragging, far from that. I have learned more from my students than any school or university could ever teach me. I would like to share just a few examples of student reactions from my teaching ***that I did not seek out or expected***. Perhaps some of these experiences will be helpful as you possibly consider teaching as a vocation.

Like most teachers and professors, we don't often hear much if anything from students about what they have gained from teaching them. Many career teachers and professors go about their tasks working hard for their students with the goal they are understanding and growing intellectually. Some colleges and universities have end of course assessments students can fill out and hopefully students will be frank about the class and what has or has not been learned. At other unexpected times students can share what's on their minds and completely surprise a teacher or professor.

One such insistent took place in Tucson, Arizona in a hospital educational setting for emotionally handicapped students. One teenage native American girl was having a lot of adjustment problems associating with others after being abused in her home. She was reluctantly hospitalized for her emotional problems. After a lengthy period of work and counseling she made an amazing turn around and began to blossom and became a great student. She was transferred to a relative's home and was readmitted to public high school. Reports indicated she was doing very well and was planning to attend college.

About a year later I received an invitation to attend her high school graduation, enclosed was a wonderful note where she detailed how important my classroom had been for her. *I was very surprised* and couldn't really remember any specific action I had taken that was so helpful to her. We did work hard at learning to listen to students during classroom sessions and perhaps that was all that she needed. All of the hospitalized students attended daily counseling sessions of which I was not a part but what went on in class was often discussed. We would get feedback from these counseling sessions and then update teaching procedures to help students that needed more support.

I could not attend the native American girl's high school graduation as I had just gone back to active duty in the Air Force for a short tour of duty. I sent her card and letter stating how happy I was knowing she was doing so well and enclosed a nice gift. Since I was a state certified teacher with several subject endorsements the students were not held back a grade when they returned to public school. Many students were gradually assimilated back to public school during a month-long period and also had family counseling sessions set up as needed to help parents with their returning family members.

On my first day as a teacher at the psychiatric hospital, I was introduced as the new teacher and was immediately surrounded by four boys who had many problems. I had a very large and muscular psychiatric technician who assisted me in keeping order, his name was Charlie, and he was excellent with all the students and did not tolerate any misbehavior.

The boys said they didn't like me and that I was just a "Dic- head"!

My response was to shake each of the boy's hand and as I looked them all right in the eyes, I said, "I appreciate you letting me know how you feel and was happy to meet all of them and hoped they would be able to learn a lot in my classes."

When I left that afternoon, I sat for a moment in my Jeep before driving home and said to myself, "What have you gotten yourself into Bob."

Unfortunately, in these days of high insurance costs and limited funding for long term psychiatric hospitalizations many youth needing long-term care is limited to not even available, leaving families to fend for themselves with sporadic to no counseling sessions in many insurance plans.

Some students were brought into the hospital by law enforcement, on one such occasion I was told to go to the hospital's central office and pick up a new student, a boy who was 14 years old. As I got there, he was with a Sherrif's deputy in handcuffs and ankle shackles. The deputy said he would help escort him back to the youth unit, but I refused. How would it look for me to bring a new hand cuffed and shackled student to his room with law enforcement?

I asked him to remove the handcuffs and ankle bracelets, he said, "Do you know what you're doing?"

I said yes, so he removed all of that at which time I shook his hand and introduced myself, "I'm Dr. Bob Shanks your teacher" and said, "We are now going to walk down the hall to the youth unit", he looked amazed.

"Ok."

We got along fine after that, and he was a very bright individual. He began to make slow steady progress not only academically but behaviorally as well.

We had four psychiatrists assigned to the hospital and after one of their meetings one of the staff who attended them said they were discussing the scope of weekly counseling sessions and how to improve it when one of the doctors said the only real day to day counseling that was going on was in Dr. Bob's classroom. The reason I was called "Dr. Bob" was when I started, they could not get my full name on the hospital name tag, "Dr. Robert D. Shanks Jr." so they simply put "Dr. Bob Shanks." This worked out great because as one of the psychiatrists I worked with said I still had the formality of "Dr." but also the informality of my first name "Bob". I have always believed that simple name tag did more for my acceptance as the student's teacher than anything else initially.

Sometimes, when a student was becoming out of control behaviorally, they could be sent to the Behavior Control Room (BCR) where they could be placed in a variety of restraints if needed.

On one occasion a young student was getting out of control so the psychologist on duty that day just said, "Send Dr. Bob to talk him down."

I did successfully help him, often one of my comments to students was simply, "What's the purpose of that behavior?"

He was bright enough as the question sunk into his head, so he began to calm down and relate to why he was angry.

We always had at least 10 to 15 students in our classroom. One particularly behaviorally involved young boy that was 13 years old, as I remember his name was Brian, and he was making outstanding progress. We had an indoor patio set up outside the locked down youth unit and students could work their way up to free time to have a soda and snack.

One day Brian asked to talk to me, I said "Ok."

As we sat down, I was giving him lots of positive feedback, he told me why he wanted to talk to me.

All he said was "Dr. Bob, will you adopt me."

Of course, I was completely shocked, amazed, and tried to explain to him that since I was single man trying to adopt a child was not really possible because I was also in the Air Force Reserve and was often called to short term active-duty assignments. Apparently, I was only one of a few positive male role models he had ever had. We discussed what options he had when he was to be released and I told him I would stay connected with him. Brian eventually and successfully transitioned back to his home and into public school. He and his family took advantage of the family counseling sessions as well. The last I heard about him was he was in high school succeeding academically and out for sports.

On another military assignment to the Balkans, I was assigned to work from the U.S. Embassy helping the

Albanian military in a transition to democracy. The country had been under communism for many years and was struggling as it began to emerge into a democratically free country. As an intelligence analyst I was assigned to a team of military advisors made up of one Army, one Navy, one Marine and myself as the Air Force representative.

We were all under the supervision of the United States European Command (USEUCOM) located in Stuttgart Germany working with the U.S. Ambassador, and State Department representatives at the Embassy compound in Tirana, Albania. One of my main jobs was serving as a liaison to the Albanian Central Military hospital helping it to transition into western medical practices. The hospital was extremely limited in its scope of treatment practices and equipment. We had teams of experts coming in from Germany to assist the hospital in learning how to operate new equipment and understand newer western medical procedures.

One day I received a call from the Ambassador who wanted to visit with me briefly. He had learned I had been a teacher and professor and had worked at a psychiatric hospital.

My thought immediately was, "What did I do to be called into the Ambassador's office and what did he want?"

We discussed his role and the many complexities of being an ambassador in a poor and developing third-world country struggling to emerge into democracy. There were a number of Albanian pilots at the airport who flew a variety of Russian Mig aircraft but knew little to no English. Of course, English is the language of aviation so to fly out of Albania into other areas of Europe proficiency in English is a requirement. He asked me if I could teach a small group of Albanian pilots English. I had taught English and journalism in public school but not to adults and that was not my main military job in my assignment to Albania. I respectfully declined but he had already sought permission from our U.S. European command headquarters in Germany so like it or not I had a new twice a week job of teaching English to a small group of six Albanian pilots. My Army Officer in Charge (OIC) of our small group of American military advisors was not at all happy with my new assignment. My OIC was a full colonel, I was a Lt. Col. at the time.

I had to really scramble to get some teaching supplies, books and figure out just what I could do in such short periods of time and what kind of English books can I obtain, and a way to begin teaching English to a small group of adult pilots in a very poor Balkan country with frequent power outages, poor infrastructure, limited water availability and poor transportation. The very first class was held at the Albanian Ministry of Defense building in central Tirana, Albania. While I thought it would be a very small group of five or six pilots, I was shocked as the pilots brought their families, so the classroom was full. I was fortunate to have a very capable Albanian interpreter to assist me in this very daunting task.

Teaching is indeed a way to begin to make a small difference here and there in our topsy-turvy often politically charged environment in our country. In the main scheme of rewarding jobs, teaching does stand out as a critically important job that can "move mountains" so to speak and can break down all kinds of barriers. Like most people, I can think of a few teachers and professors in my life that really impressed me and made a difference in my life's direction. Author Trey Gowdy's recommendation to youth wanting to make a difference was to go into teaching is a good recommendation. However, when comparing wages, it is evident that many teaching jobs don't offer the kind of salaries many are looking for after graduation from college. One has to decide and then stick to whatever vocational plan is chosen.

Being a teacher and professor in my life has indeed provided me with many great memories and experiences. I did try to make a small difference here and there in my life with teaching as the cornerstone in my career. Even though I was an intelligence analyst and worked in the intelligence field in my military career, teaching has provided me with some outstanding experiences over the years. I would not change anything if I had to do it all over again.

A Defining and Interesting Early Military Experience

One of my assignments I had while at Kirtland AFB in New Mexico was to load 35mm film into a high-speed drum camera to photograph high voltage discharges into various materials to see how they tolerated these explosive discharges. I worked in a large cage lined with safety wire called a Faraday Cage to protect those inside from stray electromagnetic discharges. I was to fire the electronic discharge when a red light was on, it blinked as the drum passed behind the lens of the high-speed camera so we could see a sequence of how the material behaved as it exploded due to the high voltage discharges. I would then unload the film for processing in the darkroom and then the scientists and engineers would examine each frame showing how the material handled the charge as it exploded. They were examining materials for space flight and reentry vehicles. Other research and developmental projects were often brought into the photo lab for studio photography. The lab had a complete black and white laboratory as well as a color lab. The lab also had a well-developed aerial photography section for filming in-flight tests and other testing requiring motion pictures.

The Air Force had at least one of every operational aircraft at the time (early 1960s) assigned to the 4925 Test Group (A) to develop various needed systems. The "A" was for Atomic and indicated extensive research was also going on in nuclear energy, so we all had to wear dosimeters and have them checked at regular intervals for radiation exposure depending on where one worked, however, no one in the photo section was ever exposed to excessive radiation. All personnel at the base had badges with all the areas on the base designated and marked specifically as to the areas they were allowed entry based on the type of job. The photo personnel were assigned to what then was designated as "Area E" and were allowed to enter many other areas to do photography. Being assigned to the photo section allowed photo staff entry to almost every area despite other restrictions.

Being assigned to a research and development group as a young, enlisted guy from the plains of Nebraska on an active Air Force base was a blessing as I was exposed to so many exciting aviation developments and innovations that were underway in the early 1960s. Seeing aviation history taking place never fully sunk into my young mind but seeing all the space flight research and other developments underway I then realized I had to go to college somehow when my four years of enlisted service was over.

UFOs or UAPs Just What are They?

Here is some general information on Unknown Aerial Phenomenon (UAP) or Unidentified Flying Objects (UFO). Much of the information here is from the program Contact, produced for the Discovery Channel, with Nick Karnaze, a retired Marine intelligence officer, and international space journalist Sarah Cruddas.

A lot of information on UAPs/UFOs has been gathered and discussed not only in the printed media but also on television documentary programs. One recent program was on the Discovery Channel and featured a retired Marine, intelligence officer, Nick Karnaze, and international space journalist Sarah Cruddas efforts to track down good solid information on all types of unexplained aerial phenomenon. They interviewed a number of reliable witnesses and a host of well-known and respected scientists and other related experts. Their travels took them all over the country and internationally. Karnaze recently related in a previous interview, he had his own sighting with a cigar-shaped UFO when on active duty. He also said that some of the UAP/UFO data collected seems to indicate a correlation between UAP/UFO sightings and natural disasters. The question emerged from the program that these sightings could be something "beyond" a classified military program.

Within the last couple of years, it was discovered the U.S. has a program here solely tasked with investigating these phenomena entitled Advanced Aerospace Threat Identification Program (AATIP), formerly highly classified. Not only here but other countries have similar programs, some not revealed, and some denied to even exist. One international program is Chile's Committee for the Study of Anomalous Aerial Phenomenon (**CEFAA**).

Chile has had a flurry of documented UAP/UFO activities for years. Colbun Lake in Central Chile had officials there document the strange vanishing of tons of water from that large lake in the mountains after several sightings of UAPs/UFOs over the lake. The water level mysteriously dropped over two feet mystifying Chilean officials, scientists, and experts. No logical scientific reason could be found for the water suddenly disappearing.

Is there a correlation to the UAP/UFO's? How can that theory even be proved? [1]

The Discovery Channel "Contact" program was filmed at several locations in the U.S. as well as in Chile. They interviewed countless scientists and aviation experts here as well as abroad. Included in the program's data was information from NASA, the CIA, and other U.S. Federal agencies. One interesting item that has repeatedly been well documented is the fact there are more UAP/UFO sightings near volcanoes. Some concentrated sightings can also center on or around military sites, ICBM launch sites, and nuclear facilities for some unknown reason.

A private group that investigates UAP/UFO sightings is the mutual UFO Network (MUFON). This group is seriously engaged in the scientific study of these phenomenon. Anyone can become a member. Visit the web site if interested. According to **MUFON**, "The modern UFO mystery has three modern traceable roots: the late 19th century 'mystery airships' reported in the newspapers of the western United States, 'foo fighters' reported by

---

[1] (EN.CEFAA.GOB, n.d.)

Allied aviators during World War II and the Kenneth Arnold 'flying saucer' sighting near Mt. Rainier, Washington on June 24, 1947."[2]

This writer has never seen a UAP/UFO; however, they are flying phenomena many reliable aviation experts and scientists have seen in our skies around the U.S. and worldwide for decades. It's fine to be skeptical but from a scientific point of view skepticism can easily turn into cynicism which runs counter to scientific inquiry and discovery.

---

[2] (MUFON, n.d.)

The Mystic and Wonder of Unidentifed Aerial Phenomenon (UAP)

Better Known in the Past as Unidentified Flying Objects (UFO)

There is a wide variety of articles, photos and other scientific research including wild theories on the "Flying Saucer" phenomenon. What the author of this essay believes is not important. This article is because of the author's interest in unidentified flying objects seen flying in our atmosphere and reported in the media here and world wide that cannot be fully explained.

For years the U.S. government denied the existence of these strange flying objects seen around the world but now has done an amazing about-face and is starting to more seriously study these flying objects. Because of this government denial and the resulting backlash of rediculed if you believed in UFO's the transistion from the acronym UFO to Unidentified Aerial Phenomenon (UAP) has helped restore some scientific credibility to finding out just what these aerial phenomena really are. Other countries have been more open to serious investigations of UFO/UAPs, particularly in South America.

Part of the confusing problem with UAPs and UFOs in the past, is all of these ideas and theories have been hyjacked for movies, books and othe fictional entertainment. So what is scientific data and what isin't can make it a difficult topic to handle with credibility. Some well trained and educated individuals in the scientific community see the acronymns UFO or UAP and immediately become skeptical and subcounciously seem to refuse to consider whether there can be any new science developed or discovered. Even some very credible scientists such as Search for Estraterretrial Intelligence (SETI) astronomer Seth Shostak have made disparaging remarks about UFOs and UAPs without even attempting to include any data to validate their remarks.

Adding to the confusion are individuals like the discredited Bob Lazar who has made claims he worked for the government on UFOs but no record can be found of his involvement further hampers real scientific growth in information on determining just what are people seeing. Then there are the wild movies, alien apduction stories and other fantasies. Trying to get an accurate perspective on just what unidentified aerial phenomenon are becomes challenging, difficult and almost impossible.

This writer's opinion is that some TV programs on the Science and History Channels actually are beneficial in helping to remove the negative stigma associated with UFO and UAP sightings. Well researched and produced programs like Giorgio A. Tsokalos Ancient Aliens program and the History Channel's program on what some South American Countries are doing in researching UAPs adds scientific credibility. Former US Army Counter

Intelligence operative Luis Elizondo had also been featured on various news programs as well sharing his experiences with UAPs. Believe it or not even some politicians have even added credibility bringing this to the publics attention. The NASA program "Unexplained Files" has been a surprising rational focus on UAPs.

The Project Blue Book was the initial start in the right direction in the 1950's. So whether you agree or disagree on just what UAPs are or are not, keep looking for stories and data as a matter of curiosity as as well as a national security interest.

Pentagon's Plan in Case Alien's Discovered

The Pentagon says it hasn't found aliens — but it does have a plan just in case aliens are discovered. On Wednesday April 19, 2023, the Senate Armed Services Committee met with the individual in charge of keeping track of UFOs for the Pentagon. Sean Kirkpatrick, head of the Department of Defense's All-domain Anomaly Resolution Office (ARRO), testified that, yes, there have indeed been numerous documented instances of unidentified aerial phenomena. At least so far, though, there's no evidence that any of the encounters Kirkpatrick's team has studied are in any way related to visitors from another planet.

"In our research, ARRO has found no credible evidence thus far of extraterrestrial activity, off-world technology or objects that defy the known laws of [3]physics," said Kirkpatrick. However, there is a plan in place if alien activity is ever discovered.

---

[3] (aol.com/news, n.d.)

Kirkpatrick testified, "In the event sufficient scientific data were ever obtained that a UAP encountered can only be explained by extraterrestrial origin, we are committed to working with our interagency partners at NASA to appropriately inform the U.S. government's leadership of its findings. "Now, does that mean the general public would find out? Your guess is as good as anyone's.

The person in charge of the Pentagon's efforts to study UFOs told members of the U.S. Senate at a Wednesday hearing that he has no evidence they come from outer space.

Three members of the Senate Armed Services committee heard testimony from Sean Kirkpatrick, director of the All-domain Anomaly Resolution Office. AARO was formed last year by the Pentagon to help study unidentified aerial phenomena, or UAP, the government's preferred term for mysterious objects seen in the sky.

Astronomer with a telescope gazing at the night sky. (Getty images)

"This is a hunt mission for what [somebody might] be doing in our backyard that we don't know about," said Kirkpatrick, who added that the goal was to set a standard across the entire Department of Defense for this type of investigation.

Kirkpatrick spent much of the hearing discussing the logistics of his organization's process, their work with other agencies and their progress in meeting benchmarks set by Congress. But he did present examples of UAPs they had studied, including a small sphere zipping over the Middle East that Kirkpatrick conceded would "be virtually impossible to fully identify" based only on the video.

While Kirkpatrick said his group hasn't been able to identify every encounter it has studied, it hadn't found any evidence that visitors from another planet were responsible for any of them.

"I should also state clearly for the record that in our research, ARRO has found no credible evidence thus far of extraterrestrial activity, off-world technology or objects that defy the known laws of physics," Kirkpatrick said.

Sean Kirkpatrick (Department of Defense)

However, Kirkpatrick did say there was a plan in place should evidence of an alien technology arise, stating, "In the event sufficient scientific data were ever obtained that a UAP encountered can only be explained by extraterrestrial origin, we are committed to working with our interagency partners at NASA to appropriately inform U.S. government's leadership of its findings."

Kirkpatrick showed a chart with reporting trends of anomalies from 1996 to 2023, which found that most sightings were of a round object, one to four meters in length and typically white, silver, or translucent, at an altitude between 10,000 and 30,000 feet with no thermal exhaust detected.

The sightings were clustered along the East and West coasts of the United States, in the Middle East and near Japan and the Korean peninsula.

Sen. Kirsten Gillibrand, D-N.Y. (Getty Images)

The hearing, chaired by Sen. Kirsten Gillibrand, D-N.Y., also addressed what Kirkpatrick and the senators viewed as potential threats from China and Russia, citing the incident earlier this year when a Chinese weather balloon crossed over the continental United States and the series of UAPs that were shot down in the immediate aftermath.

Sen. Joni Ernst, R-Iowa, asked Kirkpatrick if Chinese or Russian technology was responsible for any of the sightings. Kirkpatrick said that while the two countries have technology on par or ahead of the United States, it is "really hard" to know "if what we observe doesn't have a Chinese or Russian flag on the side of it."

"Are there capabilities that could be employed against us in both [as in surveillance] and a weapons fashion?" Kirkpatrick said. "Absolutely. Do I have evidence that they're doing it in these cases? No, but I have concerning indicators."

The hearing followed a 2021 Department of Defense report on UAPs that found 144 sightings dating back to 2004 as well as a May 2022 House Intelligence panel that was the first Congressional hearing on the topic in more than 50 years. Rep. Andre Carson, D-Ind., who chaired it, said, "Unidentified aerial phenomena are a potential national security threat, and they need to be treated that way.

"For too long, the stigma associated with UAPs has gotten in the way of good intelligence analysis," he added. "Pilots avoided reporting or were laughed at when they did. [Pentagon] officials relegated the issues to the back room or swept it under the rug entirely, fearful of a skeptical national security community.

"Today we know better," Carson continued. "UAPs are unexplained, it's true, but they are real. They need to be investigated, and any threats they pose need to be mitigated."

During his testimony Wednesday, Kirkpatrick said that anyone with alternate theories should submit them to credible scientific journals, stating, "that is how science works, not by blog or social media." Kirkpatrick added that the goal of his agency was to attempt to balance transparency with protecting the secrets of the U.S. military and the intelligence community.

"By its very nature, the UAP challenge has for decades lent itself to mystery, sensationalism and even conspiracy," Kirkpatrick said. "For that reason, ARRO remains committed to transparency, accountability and to sharing as much with the American public as we can, consistent with our obligation to protect not only intelligence sources and methods but U.S. and allied capabilities.

Protesters march in Washington, D.C., in 1995 to raise awareness about a weather balloon crash. at Roswell, N.M., in 1947. (Joshua Roberts/AFP via Getty Images)

The military has had an interest in UFOs since at least the 1940s. In 1952, the Air Force set up Project Blue Book, a classified program that counted more than 12,000 UFO sightings over its 17-year existence, with hundreds still unexplained.

In a March 1966 letter to two fellow congressmen, then-Rep. Gerald Ford wrote, "In the firm belief that the American public deserve a better explanation than that thus far given by the Air Force, I strongly recommend that there be a committee investigation of the UFO phenomena. I think we owe it to the people to establish credibility regarding UFOs and to produce the greatest possible enlightenment on this subject."

The following month, Ford issued a statement saying that while some had "ridiculed" his call for a congressional investigation, there were a fraction of those who supported looking into a March event in which 40 people, including 12 police officers, claimed to have seen a cluster of UFOs.

In 2017, the New York Times published a story about how former Senate Majority Leader Harry Reid, D-Nev., had pushed for funding for the Advanced

Aerospace Threat Identification Program (AATP), which investigated unexplained aerial sightings. The program ran from 2007 to 2012.

"I'm not embarrassed or ashamed or sorry I got this thing going," said Reid. "I think it's one of the good things I did in my congressional service. I've done something that no one has done before."

Problem Solving Steps - A Key to Success

Sometimes the problems one must confront at work can seem overwhelming. The symptoms of a problem can cause a lot of havoc, wasted time and energy. If not careful too much time can be spent on the symptomatic results of a problem. The first order of business then is to define the problem by identifying and analyzing the cause or causes of a problem. Once the root causes of a problem are discovered solutions can then be explored. There are basically four steps involved in problem solving.

The first step is of course specifically defining the problem so your focus will be on the problem and not the symptoms resulting from the problem. These steps outlined here are of a general nature. The discussion here on problem solving is generic so adapt and modify to fit your situation or situations and evaluate other methods as well.

Step One – Define the Problem

There are many charts and methods for tackling problems, so do a little research and pick a method or chart you feel comfortable using. Pick several examples and identify the key steps, adapt them for your situation or situations. Document who does what, review policies and procedures and try to determine what the outcomes should be.

Step Two – Generate Alternative Solutions

Always try to develop several alternative solutions before evaluating any of them and don't discuss them yet. Don't make the mistake of trying to hurriedly pick a solution that sounds workable. Don't just focus on trying to get the results you want. Waiting until several solutions can be discussed may open doors for learning something new that will allow for real improvement. Brainstorming and team problem-solving techniques are both useful tools in this stage of problem solving.

Step Three-Evaluate and Select an Alternative Solution

When evaluating solutions, one must be careful not to have an alternative being discussed cause other unanticipated problems if too hurriedly adopted. All appropriate individuals involved must be given a chance to input concerns and ideas. As alternatives are discussed, they should be evaluated as to whether they fit within the organization's goals and objectives. Should alternatives be selected for testing if feasible is a question to consider if possible. Keeping key personnel involved will help with the acceptance of whatever alternative is selected.

Step Four-Implement and Follow-up on the Alternative Selected

The leaders of a company or business may be tasked with the implementation of a solution. Hopefully, the involvement of others in the development of a solution will help as some staff will have a sense of ownership and involvement so it can be more easily "sold" to other staff members and workers.

This involvement of other key staff members will also help to minimize resistance to the subsequent changes because perhaps not everyone agreed with the changes. Involvement of others will also help in establishing positive feedback for monitoring the solution is important.

Again, this is a generic discussion of a possible problem-solving technique. Do your own research as mentioned earlier so adapt a portion or parts of the many models for problem solving that exist to fit your particular issue.

What is the Difference Between Measurement, Assessment and Evaluation In Education?

Having been a public-school teacher as well as a civilian and military university professor, I was always interested in how to evaluate if students were learning. The question in the title of this essay is a critical one that students, no matter whether they are in high school or college, should be able answer. Many students seem to struggle with answering the simple question, what does it mean to understand? One of the key aspects of understanding is the sentence, **"not understood at all..."** (If something is not understood in more than one way it is not fully understood at all.)

Measurement, assessment, and evaluation are key aspects of statistics, yet each one has a very different meaning. Future teachers should understand these concepts as should all college students. Other detailed information can be found at http://www.adprima.com/. Dr. Bob Kizlik covers a lot of curriculum development concepts there. Dr.

organization is located near Philadelphia, Pennsylvania. Much of this short article is based on his research and descriptions of these terms. Dr. Kizlik uses this sentence above about learning and understanding to begin his discussion of these important statistical terms and learning. I think it is important for authors and writers to understand these terms as well.

Measurement refers to the process of determining the physical dimensions of an object. One exception, however, is the use of this word to determine the IQ of a person. The phrase "this test measures IQ" is commonly used by educators. The application of a standard scale or measuring method is used for behavioral measurement in education. So, then the word assessment is quite different from measurement when used in education.

Assessment is the process of obtaining information relative to some known objective or goal. In teaching, educators assess at the end of a lesson or unit to determine the information gained by students. Assessment then is just another way of saying a test. Assessment of understanding is much more difficult and complex. Skills can be practiced; understanding cannot especially when trying to demonstrate something has been learned and understood in more than one way.

Evaluation is the most complex and least understood of these terms. When we evaluate, we seek information to make judgments about what has been learned in a given situation (often using objectives, goals, standards, and procedures). In education, we classify objects, situations, people, and conditions. ***In summation, we measure distance, we assess learning, and we evaluate results in terms of some set of criteria.*** The three terms are connected but must be thought of as separate but connected in related ideas and processes used in a given learning situation.

Measurement, assessment and evaluation is also a part of the processes used in science to determine whether or not something is true and/or has value. Scientists formulate hypotheses or educated guesses about the relationship between or among the different facets of knowledge.

Assessment refers to the collection of data, measurement is the process of quantifying data, research refers to the use of data to describe, predict and better understand whatever phenomena is under consideration for testing and evaluation.

All of this information here is a general-purpose method for judging worth or quality. Hopefully, this has been a discussion as a beginning of understanding in general so learning will be done and understood in more than one way.

The Art of Asking Good Questions

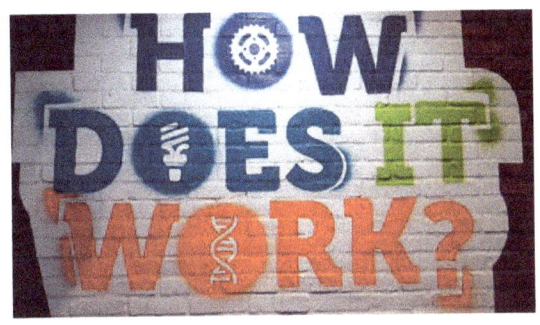

It makes no difference the profession one has chosen, it is still an important attribute to learn the art of asking good questions. Good questions promote thinking and can generate good discussions. While this is an important technique for teaching and educators to master, it has considerable value in a host of professions to generate critical thinking and promote a high degree of professionalism. The art of Socratic questioning and critical thinking was part of Socrates methods, the ancient Greek Philosopher who lived from 469-399 B.C.

Keep in mind that critical thinking and Socratic questioning both seek meaning and truth, so the art of questioning is important to developing excellent thinking abilities. Socrates stressed the importance of probing an individual's thinking and knowledge. He believed that acknowledging what one didn't know or understand was important to the goal of focusing on what should be done or understood about a problem or topic. Socrates stressed to his students that a lack of knowledge is not a bad thing but a key to developing a higher level of understanding. The skill of problem solving needed to understand what must be done to make known what is unknown is important so knowledge can be gained, and problems solved. ***This is critical thinking***. Critical thinking can provide intellectual tools to re-direct a person's thinking to gain knowledge and solve problems.

Educational reformer, John Dewey, labeled this as reflective inquiry where the individual thinker studies a subject or problem so action can be taken to re-direct or refocus thinking for problem solving and gaining knowledge through disciplined questioning.

As one uses this type of detailed and disciplined questioning all alternative points of view are considered to possibly develop new knowledge and skills to solve a variety of problems and issues. Over the years there have been many educational studies that the level of thinking and problem solving can significantly improve through critical thinking and thoughtful detailed questioning.

The importance of developing complex thinking and questioning abilities for learning and problem solving is a critical skill for anyone to master and study no matter what the profession. Mastering Socratic questioning and critical thinking can be an important self-directed goal and anyone to achieve.

To become better at critical thinking, one must be curious and want to explore new knowledge and solutions to problems and work at developing good questions to distinguish between what is fact and what is opinion.

The Importance of Critical Thinking in Today's Topsey-Turvey Educational Systems

One cannot diminish the importance of critical thinking in today's educational systems, from K to 12 as well as at all levels of college and university education. A simple review of all the tactics taught and needed to function into days world, one soon realizes the oldest and most powerful teaching tactic for fostering critical thinking is  the ancient well-tested Socratic teaching techniques.

The development of logical reasoning and disciplined thought is what Socratic questioning is all about no matter what subject is being discussed or evaluated whether in a school or in the real world of work. This concept is valuable for study by all students, and anyone interested in understanding the history and importance of

Socratic questioning. He is considered the founding figure of Western philosophy (469-399 BC). Socrates has been described as one of the strangest of the Greek philosophers. He grew up during the golden age of Pericles' Athens and served with distinction as a Greek soldier.

Socrates is best known as a questioner of everything and everyone. There is a lot of information online and in libraries about the Socratic Method of fostering critical thinking. The aim of questioning is to probe the underlying beliefs upon which each participant's statements, arguments and assumptions are built.

The abilities we gain by focusing on the elements of reasoning in a disciplined and self-assessing way, and the logical relationships that result from such disciplined thought, prepare us for Socratic questioning.

Thankfully, there is a predictable set of relationships that hold for all subjects and disciplines. This is given in the general logic of reasoning, since every subject has been developed by those who have shared goals, problems, and how to interpret, organize and begin to collectively examine solutions and purposes. All individuals then can share and discuss alternative points of view and how to move forward. Sounds easy but it is not and requires a lot of cooperation and work by all individuals involved in the process.

At each step in the process, all involved can probe into the nature of the questions, problem or issue that is of concern. All participants should strive to ensure that all relevant data and information is available for consideration. Critical thinking is sophisticated brain work and requires a lot of planning and thinking.

Critical thinking represents a dimension into which one can delve into as a questioning and critical thinking person. We can question goals and purposes. We can probe into the nature of the question, problem, or issue that is on the floor. We can inquire into whether we have all the relevant data and information. We can consider alternative interpretations of the data and information. We can analyze key concepts and ideas. We can question assumptions being made. We can ask all involved to trace out the implications and consequences of what they are saying. We can consider alternative points of view. All of these, and more, are the proper focuses of the Socratic questioner.

Write Something That Means Something Based on Verifiable Factual Information

We live in an age of almost instant communications due to the Internet and smart phones that everyone seems to use. Consequently, the public needs to have a degree of skepticism when accessing information circulating via various Internet programs or whatever email program one is using. Publications being read should also be subject to the reader's critical eye. Due to our freedoms in the U.S. our election periods can have information that almost seems meaningless and can have little or no foundation in truth, both the Democrat and Republican parties have used politically charged information in our country's history. It is critically important that all information should be verifiable using at least three sources.

When verifying information, a variety of sources should be used, if possible, depending on the situation or circumstances surrounding a quote, data, or information being sent out via the Internet. Often, newspapers and other print publications do not do a particularly good job of verifying what they are publishing. So be wary of information if something just does not seem correct or seems just too amazing.

During the 19th Century the term "yellow journalism" described the style of news reporting that emphasized sensationalism over facts. The modern-day version of yellow journalism is "clickbait" to get people to click on an internet link for reviews to generate profits. Clickbait and yellow journalism use sensationalism, exaggeration and fabrication, lack of verification, personal attacks, scandals, a lack of journalistic credibility for facts, and ethical concerns often emphasizing social and political divisions. A controversial practice sometimes used is called "checkbook journalism" where unethical news reporters pay sources for their information without verifying its truth. Checkbook journalism can turn politicians and celebrities into lucrative targets of unproven allegations. The news is filled with reports of lawsuits, legal actions, and other allegations of wrongdoing these days involving political or famous individuals.

Do the work, verify information, stick to the facts, and follow them wherever they may lead, to assist in getting to the truth of a situation. Checking the facts is a pillar of support for journalism when practiced correctly and entails demanding work. So too then, the reader or individual getting the report should also be ready to question and verify the information.

When reading a newspaper, listening to the news, or accessing the news using whatever method or methods one likes to use, have a critical eye and a sense of skepticism, especially if no sources or attribution is being used in the report. Be quick to question the accuracy and be ready to double check the information if deemed important or critical for you, your company or family. If one wants to be a journalist, be ready to ask tough questions. When you hear a politician or celebrity say "no comment" the journalist is probably on the right track in getting to the truth of a situation.

The Five Levels of Situational Awareness

The discipline part of practicing situational awareness refers to the conscious effort required to pay attention to surrounding events as well as to gut feelings even while you are busy with daily life. Scott Stewart at Strategic Forecasting.com listed five levels of awareness in his guide to Situational Awareness that covers the human condition of awareness quite well. 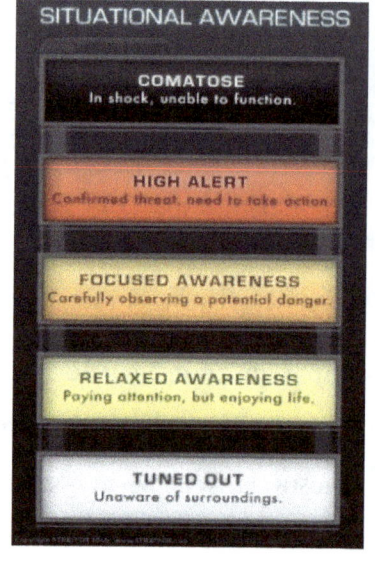 The levels are "tuned out", "relaxed awareness", "focused awareness", "high alert" and "comatose".

Before we examine these levels of awareness, it is important to remember, Situational Awareness is not a hard skill but a mindset. This is not something only practiced by highly trained police officers or special agents use, it can become a part of anyone's daily routine. This is a valuable mindset that fits well with what is often said by police and other officials, "If you see something, say something". All kinds of threats can exist, so blatant inattention, apathy, denial, and complacency can be deadly. One must practice being observant and understand the need to take responsibility for one's own security. Terrorism and criminal actions can happen, often when least expected and in unusual circumstances.

Often, a person's subconscious mind can notice subtle signs of danger that the conscious mind has trouble quantifying or even articulating. Many victims of crime or terrorism have related the experience of feeling danger prior to an incident but ignored them and later wished they had paid more attention. Trust your gut feelings and avoid potentially dangerous situations. One may experience a bit of inconvenience but never ignore these feelings as they can lead to serious trouble. Let's examine these levels mentioned above.

The first level, "tuned out" is a basic environment experienced by everyone, as an example when driving your mind can focus on other things while driving automatically. The next level is "relaxed awareness" where one is relaxed but watching closely what's going on around you. "Focused awareness" is a higher level of concentration like driving in hazardous weather. As we move up the continuum of awareness, the next level is "high alert" but one can still function, but the environment is scary. The last level of awareness is the "Comatose level" when individuals are so petrified that they are in such a panic-induced state all response to stimuli stops.

The body and mind require rest, but the higher levels of awareness take a lot of energy. We all need to be aware of these levels and understand how they work. This is why law enforcement, and military personnel receive so much training in situational awareness.

It's important to stress that the study of situational awareness does not mean being paranoid or obsessively concerned about security. The process of understanding situational awareness is critical these days, especially in view of increased U.S. State Department travel advisories issued for Americans traveling abroad. Even at home, we all should be aware of our surroundings and practice Situational Awareness.

Finding the Right Level Of Situational Awareness

I have discussed the levels of situational awareness in my past essays, so I need to discuss identifying what level is ideal at any given time. We are all aware of the fact the body and mind both require rest, so we all must spend several hours each day at the "comatose level" while we sleep.

Increased technology doesn't increase situational awareness.

www.chaincartoons.com

When we are sitting in our homes, watching television, or reading a book it is appropriate to operate in the "tuned-out" mode. We must guard against falling into this mode or operating "tuned-out" at inappropriate times such as being on a dark street at night in a potentially dangerous area or while driving.

Some people have developed the mindset that crime or potential threats can't happen to me. Consider carefully where you are and always be alert to potential threats. Learn to be observant of your surroundings at all times to whatever degree the situation might require, especially while driving. Let's briefly discuss what it means to find the right level of awareness based on the situation.

If you are "tuned out" while you are driving and something suddenly happens like a blow out or someone running into the road, you may have trouble reacting safely. A lack of reactions or slow reactions occurs because it is difficult to change one's mental state quickly say from "tuned out" to "high alert". In some instances, people can panic, freeze, and cannot react properly, some actually stall.

Trying to be prepared for the unexpected is difficult, while training does help people move up and down the alertness continuum, it is still quite difficult even for highly trained individuals. This is why law enforcement, and military personnel receive so much training in situational awareness. Keep in mind that situational awareness does not mean getting paranoid or overly concerned about security. No one can operate in a state of "focused awareness" for extended periods before becoming quickly tiresome and hard to maintain. "High alert" can be maintained for only brief periods of time before exhaustion begins to occur and possibly the "fight-or-flight" response sets in, this can be helpful if it can be controlled. When it gets out of control a constant stream of adrenaline and stress is not healthy for the body and mind and can hamper security and borders on becoming panicked. However, an increased level of awareness is prudent when engaging in common everyday tasks like visiting an ATM or walking to your car in a dark parking lot. High awareness can easily be shifted back to relaxed awareness.

Remember, the human body was simply not designed to operate under constant high stress for long periods of time. Everyone, even highly skilled individuals, require time to rest and recover. You can hone your awareness skills by practicing some simple drills. As an example, consciously move awareness levels up to focused awareness for short periods of time. Know the exits when entering a building, be aware of people in a restaurant or subway and paying attention to cars making the same turns you are making is easy to do with some practice.

Some law enforcement officers are trained to look at people around them and attempt to figure out their stories, moods, and what they are doing. All of this can be done by simple observation. Such awareness practice permits potential threats to be avoided if in questionable areas that might be dangerous or even in daily activities.

Worldwide Terrorism is on the Rise

Terrorism is a major concern in the mid-east but not only there but worldwide. One of the most effective ways to combat terrorism starts with understanding Situational Awareness and learning to practice it. One has to remember that this is nothing more than simple awareness, being aware of one's surroundings and identifying potential threats and dangerous situations. Situational Awareness is also a mindset, as well as a simple survival skill that anyone can develop and learn to use.

This mindset as a skill is not something that can only be practiced by highly trained agents or specialized corporate security teams. All that is needed is the will and discipline to develop this ability. The news often makes us all too aware that threats exist. Ignorance or denial of Situational Awareness can reduce a person's chances of quickly recognizing emerging threats and avoiding them. Apathy or denial of these threats in our daily lives can be deadly.

An important element for developing a proper situational mindset is one should always be aware of personal safety no matter where one lives even if living in a small community. The resources of any government are finite and cannot stop every potential terrorist attack or criminal action.

All Americans have a responsibility to look out for themselves, but also for family and neighbors. As one moves into learning this Situational Awareness mindset, trusting your "gut" feelings or intuitions is critical. Our subconscious mind can often notice subtle signs of danger that our conscious mind has difficulty understanding or articulating. Many victims who have experienced and survived dangerous incidents or situations but ignored them have related to law enforcement that it is important to pay attention to those "gut" feelings. Ignoring your subconscious mind may cause you a bit of an inconvenience but by not paying attention to those feelings could lead to serious trouble.

As terrorism continues to surge worldwide, we all need to concentrate on developing a keen discipline based on Situational Awareness. Remember it is a simple skill and mindset that can be learned and practiced unconsciously by everyone as they go about their daily activities.

The CIA is Broken - Its Main Job: Protecting the U.S. from Threats

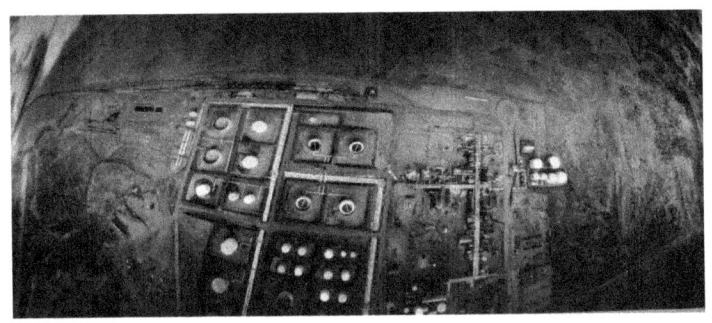

A former CIA Operations Officer, Dr. Charles S. Faddis, recently wrote an article for the Hillsdale College *"Imprimis"* publication entitled *"Why the CIA No Longer Works – and How to Fix It"*. He briefly outlines the history of the CIA as created primarily to protect the U.S. from possible surprise attacks such as occurred in WWII at Pearl Harbor and recently the 911 attacks on our country when four airliners were hijacked crashing them into four U.S. targets. There was not a single intelligence source reporting the possible 911 attacks. These attacks killed almost 3,000 Americans. Bin Laden and Al Qaeda fully understood the capabilities of American Intelligence. Bin Laden had no cell phone, he communicated with his organization via couriers dealing with them face to face. There were no emails, no text messages, or phone calls for U.S. or foreign intelligence to intercept or track. Agent Faddis further stated it took the CIA almost a decade to get a source within Al Qaeda to help track Bin Laden's location even though this was of the highest priority for the organization.

This writer, having spent a career in the intelligence field, and now a member of the Chino Valley RC Flyers serving as the newsletter editor and photographer, I felt this article really is related to RC flying from the perspective and fact a lot of intelligence and images are gained using various drones, jet aircraft as well as satellite imagery. (See cover digital photo in our December 2023 issue (www.chinovalleyflyers.org) of our field taken from a RC turbine model.) Most of the commands I served with in intelligence always had a CIA officer assigned for access to share critical intelligence as needed.

The photograph accompanying this article is a sample of a low attitude RF-4C Phantom film image of a POL gas and oil storage site taken with a low pan 180-degree scanning film camera. Of course, these days images are generated in real time using digital imaging devices on drones, aircraft, or satellites in space. A low altitude image can show much more detail generally than images taken from high altitude or space. Flying at low altitude and fast while having many advantages is also fraught with many hazards in a combat environment. One clear advantage with real time digital combat communications is the fact that critical information can be relayed quickly using satellites.

So, What's the Solution to Fixing the CIA?

Faddis says there are two reasons the CIA is broken; one is bureaucratization and politicization. According to Faddis, the CIA recruiters now seem to only look at academic degrees and language proficiency. Faddis goes on to say that the recruiters act as if anyone can be taught to conduct espionage, which is not true. Faddis points out that "A new CIA director must make it crystal clear that there is no longer business as usual." He further states that there should be zero tolerance for any involvement in domestic politics by agents and that senior officers should be removed immediately if they are involved in politics. There should be no "foot dragging" or slow rolling cases. The CIA must return to its roots to keep the U.S. safe.

U.S. Open Borders: A Serious National Security Problem

The integrity, identity, character, and unique history of a country rests within its borders. All countries require passports and usually visas for entry. All countries have their own customs authorities at border entry points as security and protection. While we in America experience unprecedented freedoms, that is not the case for most of the world. I can understand why people want to get away from violence, corruption, crime and move here, however, coming here should be done following our laws. We cannot survive as a country with unchecked immigration. We have far too many enemies that want to take this all away from us, unfortunately our political leadership in the last few years has allowed unchecked access to our borders both in the north and especially at our southern border.

The surge in illegal immigration started in 2020 reaching a crises level in 2024. There are all kinds of presidential actions that could be taken to stem this flow of unwelcome and in many cases dangerous illegal immigration. ***This should not be considered a political issue, it's a serious national security problem.*** Having served in the United States Air Force as an intelligence analyst both on active duty and in the reserve component, we were always concerned with the "bad guys" coming into our country unchecked. Current polling is showing voters are taking this border crises seriously now as it is becoming the one main issue on the minds of all voters.

With the current surge of illegal immigration, there is no way to check backgrounds, criminal histories, and medical records such as immunizations. Our schools and communities are being flooded with illegal immigrants speaking a whole host of relatively unknown languages. Sadly, it appears almost all states in America are now being considered "border states" in some fashion.

Historically, past U.S. presidents have removed illegal immigrants in large numbers. In an article by Alex Nowrasteh writing for the CATO institute* shared a table of past deportations by U.S. Presidents. This data goes back to 1892 and is based on Homeland Securities historical data. The Cato Institute author's table of deportations is on page two of this short article.

All U.S. citizens should start writing all of their Congressional representatives about this very serious national security issue. Due to the unknown number of "got aways" of those coming across the southern border, one has to ask the question, how many of these are terrorists? How many of these are hardened criminals? How many of these "got aways" were released from mental institutions in their home countries? A large number of criminals have been stopped at the border but how many dangerous individuals are now loose in our communities? The recent surge in violent crime data seems to be a result of this mass illegal immigration in many instances.

There has been some debate on whether to call these individuals "illegal" and not undocumented, however, the law is clear on this issue, if you come to this country through the border check points and have a reason to be here you are simply a legal immigrant, there is a difference in being undocumented and being illegal.

Legal immigrants are foreign-born people legally admitted to the U.S. at border check points. Undocumented Immigrants are foreign-born people who do not possess a valid visa or other immigration documentation and have stayed longer than their temporary visa permitted or came into our country illegally, or otherwise violated the terms under which they were officially admitted.

*The Cato Institute is a public policy research organization or think tank.

Removal of Illegal Immigrants by Past U.S. Presidents

Source: Department of Homeland Security and the Cato Institute Article calculations.

*Interesting observation, Barack Obama deported, by far, more illegal immigrants than any past president.

President	Removals	Removals Per Year	Political Party	Years in Office
Grover Cleveland	9,069	2,267	Democrat	4
Woodrow Wilson	162,371	20,296	Democrat	8
Franklin D. Roosevelt	171,939	13,226	Democrat	13
Harry S. Truman	140,553	20,079	Democrat	7
John F. Kennedy	23,969	7,990	Democrat	3
Lyndon B. Johnson	48,737	9,747	Democrat	5
Jimmy Carter	105,378	26,345	Democrat	4
Bill Clinton	869,646	108,706	Democrat	8
Barack Obama*	**3,066,457**	**383,307**	**Democrat**	**8**

President	Removals	Removals Per Year	Political Party	Years in Office
Benjamin Harrison	2,801	2,801	Republican	1
William McKinley	17,642	3,528	Republican	5
Theodore Roosevelt	76,390	10,913	Republican	7
William H. Taft	83,150	20,788	Republican	4
Warren G. Harding	60,652	20,217	Republican	3
Calvin Coolidge	164,913	32,983	Republican	5
Herbert Hoover	110,275	27,569	Republican	4
Dwight D. Eisenhower	110,019	13,752	Republican	8
Richard M. Nixon	81,022	16,204	Republican	5

President	Removals	Removals Per Year	Political Party	Years in Office
Gerald R. Ford	82,316	27,439	Republican	3
Ronald Reagan	168,364	21,046	Republican	8
George Bush	141,326	35,332	Republican	4
George W. Bush	2,012,539	251,567	Republican	8
Donald J. Trump	551,449	275,725	Republican	2

Military Noncombatant Evacuation Operation (NEO)

One of my jobs in the military was as an Analyst working in the Intelligence field. I was assigned to the U.S. Air Force Air Mobility Command Intelligence Center as a reservist working out of Scott AFB, IL. In various areas of unrest in the world the U.S. has to evacuate Americans out of harm's way. One such incident occurred in 1997 in the country of Albania. We often engaged in assisting in Noncombatant Evacuation Operations (NEO) Operations. The NEO operation in Albania was called Operation Silver Lake.

After I had done a short tour of duty in Tirana, Albania, I was approached by the command at AMC to assist getting information about the airport in setting up a

NEO since I had been on the ground there. I was given a satellite photo of the Tirana, Albania area and specifically the airport there. Since I was also a trained photo interpreter, I took the photo and diagramed the ingress and egress routes into and out of the airport, outlined what the various buildings there were and gave an overall evaluation of the airport for NEO use. The airport was not in very good shape and the few civilian airlines that would fly there had often said they were going to suspend service due to the poor condition of the runways. The airport is eleven miles from the center of Tirana and took about a half an hour to get there due to the poor condition of the roads at that time. Since the airport was not well maintained a suitable site to do the NEO was selected closer to Tirana and near the U.S. Embassy. Although Tirana in Albania does not have a beach, it is only a 45-minute drive or taxi ride to get to the nearest beach at Durres, Albania located on the Adriatic Sea.

So, In March 1997, U.S. Marines from the 26th Marine Expeditionary Unit conducted the evacuation of American citizens, noncombatants, and other foreign nationals from Albania due to the country's civil unrest.

The operations were conducted by the USS Nassau's (LHA-4) amphibious readiness group. Despite initial gunfire upon landing, approximately 900 people were evacuated over 13 days. Additionally, 105 Albanians were rescued  March 16-17 from unsafe and overcrowded vessels in the water. Other U.S. Navy ships involved were the USS Nashville (LPD-13) and USS Ramage (DDG-61).

American citizens are escorted to a CH-46E "Sea Knight" of the 26th Marine Expeditionary Unit.

The bottom photo is a small American child waiting to be evacuated. US Marine Corps Photos

The Noncombatant Evacuation Operations (NEO) is the ordered mandatory or authorized (voluntary) departure of civilian noncombatants and non-essential military personnel from danger in overseas countries. The Department of State (DOS) recommends an evacuation, and the Department of the Army (DOD) plans and coordinates the execution of a NEO.

Air Mobility Command (AMC) often assists and is a vital part of a NEO depending on location and aircraft needs.

Why is Christianity so Trivialized and Attacked?

Trying to be a good Christian in America is becoming more and more difficult in these days despite our First Amendment, "Congress shall make no law respecting an establishment of religion, or prohibiting the free exercise thereof, or abridging the freedom of speech, or the press; or the right of the people to peaceably assemble, and to petition the government for a redress of grievances."

The phrase "…or prohibiting the free exercise thereof…" is critical, this is why we have so many different religious faiths being practiced freely all over our country. No religion is to be hampered or limited as it is freely worshiped. However, our country is and has always been primarily Christian in nature. It doesn't take much research in our rich American history to discover our varied current practices. Our Christian heritage is well documented in American history. Drive down any street in just about any town and city in our United States of America one easily discovers a tremendous variety of large and small churches with Christian crosses that are functioning, contributing to the community, and abiding by the First Amendment.

At the beginning of this little book, this author in his message to readers, emphasized what Christianity has done for him. He has served in the military in a wide variety of countries and in many areas of our own country and he always found it amazing how easy it was to find a Christian church he could attend either on the military base or in adjacent communities.

While doing a military tour of duty in the country of Albania the author discovered a Christian church set up by American missionaries meeting in an old abandoned former communist auditorium in Tirana, Albania with no heat but the church was making a positive impact providing support for local charities and an orphanage.

One statistic used recently at a church service said there were 280 million Americans that hadn't accepted

Christ or probably don't even know much about Him or Christianity. Evangelist Franklin Graham says he believes Christianity has been attacked and marginalized by "anti-Christ" media and liberal governments in our country. He says it's time for Christians to become more active in politics.

A Pew research article found that Christians face government harassment in a staggering 124 nations. Most Americans might find that hard to believe because most Western countries are accustomed to Christians being the norm. Bigots are people who are unreasonably and illogically prejudiced against a person or people have seized on the idea it is okay to ridicule a religion that is in the minority but in some countries even "mainstream Christians" are ridiculed. In China or a Middle Eastern country spreading the gospel of Christ could get you jailed or killed.

Mainline Christians, in most research, shows they are the oldest group increasing from the average age of 45 in 2011 to 51 in 2021. Some Christian research also found that only 32 percent of teenagers from 13 to 17 identify as religious "nones", this term refers to those surveyed as selecting "none of the above". Another poll found that 36 percent of young adults 18-29 identified also as "nones" not identifying with any religious group. Some religions in America are declining rapidly, a troubling trend.

Americans are incredibly fortunate to have a constitution that established a framework for respecting religious choice. Public schools across the country should be teaching our history accurately, unfortunately some are not or are leaving history and civics out of their curriculums entirely or teaching history that is wrong and not based on good historic educational research. All schools need to teach our history with all of its mistakes and triumphs. We are indeed fortunate to have the First Amendment that guarantees us the ability to worship or not and we all should respect other Americans and their decisions regarding religion.

Short Story Section

A Strange Old Hanger at the Airport!

Driving out to the airport one sunny Saturday afternoon to work on their airplanes, Rick and fellow pilot Randy decided to explore the old hanger located in an unused area of the airport that dated back to the WWII era. Locally, stories were circulating about that old section as haunted, the old base was gone but the old hanger remained and undoubtedly saw every type of WWII airplane in its heyday. They postponed working on their planes stored at the active end of the airport until they could adequately look inside this hanger to satisfy their curiosity. The old hanger had been boarded-up for years. The ramp outside the hanger had weeds coming up through cracks in the old concrete. Just getting to that old area of the airport was a bit difficult so they parked along the road and then walked to the very strange and sad-looking old aircraft hangar.

The pilots found one side door to the hanger unlocked. As they pushed the old jammed and warped door open clouds of dust billowed up as sunlight shined down through the old hanger door windows. It took a little time for their eyes to adjust to the semi darkness in this old aircraft home, but to their amazement, it appeared as if time had stood still. If only the walls could talk, they would tell exciting stories of the bygone days of early aviation.

Power to the hanger had been disconnected years ago but they noticed, in the dim light, an old room labeled "Mission Ready Briefing." As they slowly opened the door and peered in, it was as if the room was still ready for the next flight briefing. On the far wall was a picture of *Rod Serling* advertising the old 1950s television show "The Twilight Zone". Was somebody trying to be funny"? The tattered mission-ready briefing room just added to the spookiness of the old hanger!

Everything inside the room was dusty and unused for years. As Randy and Rick looked around a bare light bulb suddenly came on and the door slammed and locked.

"Hey there's not supposed to be any power in this building" was Randy's retort. The old "Twilight Zone" picture suddenly brightened, and the words "Terminal" lit up like a lighted billboard and the arrow started blinking as if to point to the "Terminal." Rick said, *"What Terminal, where?"* Randy looked in the direction of the arrow and muttered, *"I don't think I want to cross over into any twilight zone, let's get out of here!"* Over the closed door was a small, tattered sign that said, "This way to the terminal." A small strange yellow glow was emanating from under the door of the room!

The two pilots high-tailed it to the exit door, struggling for a moment to open it but the door finally creaked open and as they hurriedly left that strange room, they glanced back at the door labeled "Terminal," that door was suddenly gone! The door had disappeared, and the lights were off again, only the bare wall remained, labeled with the strange words: the "Twilight Zone Terminal."

But there had been a door on that back wall! Where had it gone? What was going on here? Neither pilot ever spoke about that strange encounter to anyone, nor ever ventured to that side of the airport again!

The Old Tube Powered Radio Still Works

Liam was having a blast looking around in his grandmother's attic. Liam was living with his grandmother while attending high school after his parents had died in a tragic automobile accident. There were so many really cool old items in his grandmother's attic he had never seen before and was amazed at what was stored there. His grandmother had lowered the stairs from the ceiling in the garage so Liam could retrieve an old box with a set of dishes his grandmother wanted. He asked if he could explore a little, she said not to stay there too long.

Amid all the boxes of old books and photo albums, Liam found an old radio in a wooden case with a 1939 date on its back. He remembered seeing it sitting on a small table in some old family photos. It used old tubes. Liam wondered if it still worked so he lowered it down from the attic. His grandmother said she had forgotten it was still there and doubted it worked. He cleaned off all the dust and grime. The plug looked okay and even the electrical cord didn't seem to be all that worn. He plugged it in and to his surprise it was working amid crackling static and whistling noises as he turned the dial through area stations it was picking up.

The old radio from the 1930's

Liam had the perfect spot to place the radio in his bedroom on a small nightstand next to his bed and at the desk he used to do school assignments. He thought this was probably better than a TV, he could listen to music while studying.

As he tuned the radio, he found a strange station that suddenly made the old dial's light turn from a dim yellow glow to a bright green. "What's this old radio doing", was a thought racing through Liam's mind? The green dial had the years slowly scrolling by and something in the back of Liam's mind said he should pick a year. As he touched the dial the scrolling stopped. He slowly turned the dial stopping at the year 1939 the year on the back of the radio. The round ten-inch monitor instantly transformed into a small TV-like screen with scenes from the depression era flashing by. Soup lines, massive unemployment and poverty were some of the images.

Liam had heard some of his grandmother's stories about growing up in the depression, so he was transfixed at some of the images he was seeing passing by the small monitor. Could this be an opportunity for Liam to really see what his great grandmother had endured during the great depression? He hoped he wouldn't lose the pictures on the screen. Especially the one of his great grandmother Dorthea with white hair, her eyes seem to reflect all the pain she endured living through the depression of the 1930s. The sadness reflected in the time worn face spoke volumes to Liam. He only vaguely remembers seeing her lying in her death bed when he was about 4 or 5 years old and how she looked at him and said she felt so sorry he had to grow up in this time (WWII era) with all of its uncertainty and unknown dangers. Liam's town was under a curfew, no metal toys were being made and only wooden ones were available. Locally there was an ammunition plant manufacturing all kinds of ordinance for the war effort raging in Europe fighting Germany's Hitler and the Pacific against Japan.

Liam took this photo with his cell phone of his great grandmother as it scrolled by the screen.

Just as quickly as the old radio's tuning dial turned into a view into time it suddenly reverted back to the standard radio dial. What was going on here?

The old radio screen back to normal.

What kind of radio is this and what does it mean for Liam, is there a message for him on this screen? The old ammunition plant west of town is vacant now. There were stories of strange lights seen over the area as well as odd flying machines coming and going that the farmers often reported to the local authorities.

Apparently, only those living close to the plant saw these strange aerial phenomena flying in out of the plant property. One farmer had to go onto the barricaded plant grounds to round up some stray cattle. As he rode his horse by one of the large empty hangers that remained, he heard very strange noises echoing in the hanger, that sounded like someone, or something was trapped in the building. When he peered into the faded yellow window all he could see were puffs of dust swirling about.

The cattle he had rounded up were all nervous and began running away from the hanger. His horse even reared up and almost threw him off, so he quickly followed the cattle keeping them headed toward his property.

The nervous rancher knew full well after the war the plant went through extensive decontamination processes due to the hazardous wartime ordinance manufactured there and was now safe for him and his cattle. However, what the animals were sensing was a mystery and made not only the rancher but other area farmers nervous. What was it they sensed?

The old plant was placed on standby just after WWII until the 1950s when another large company moved into it to continue supporting the military's need for various large ordinances. The U.S. Air Force, Army and Marines needed bombs and rockets for their aircraft deployed to the many contingencies breaking out all over the world, so the plant was more or less constantly in some type of use. During the Korean and Vietnam wars, 500 lb and 750 lb bombs were assembled there for the Air Force.

Liam's grandmother often had a nervous response when asked about what she knew and experienced when working at the plant during WWII. She just didn't seem to want to share any information. Old grandma McCurdy, Liam's favorite, had a bomb roll off the assembly table and on to her leg at the table where she was working. While she was convalescing, she had nightmares about the large hanger where she worked but wouldn't say why or give Liam any information even after all these years had elapsed. He was quite perplexed, she said it was just probably a bad dream.

Liam had thought about dropping out of high school, it seemed to be such a waste of time but after seeing some of this old history flashing by on the suddenly transformed radio tuning dial, he was determined to stay in school and pursue his education. He had the realization that a proper education with skills was a way to help ensure his future was better than what he had seen scrolling by the screen. After that one incident the old radio worked as it always had, it was as if the old tube powered radio had sent him a message to stay in school.

Liam suddenly became more interested in studying history and began reading all he could about those difficult depression years his grandmother and great grandmother had lived through. After visiting with his high school counselor, he decided to become a history teacher. His aptitude and intelligence test scores were always remarkably high, high school suddenly took on a new meaning for him. He decided to channel his energies into studying American and international history.

As a strange twist in this tale, the radio in Liam's room suddenly just stopped working. It was almost like it only worked long enough to get a message to Liam to stay in school.

An Encounter at the Nightcrawlers Bar

In a recent trip to my home state of Nebraska to revisit some former towns and areas that were hang outs for family, friends, and high school buddies; we ventured to a small town in central Nebraska named Worms. Yup, that's its name and in this small town of Worms is a bar aptly named the "Nightcrawlers Bar". This little bar is nestled in the heart of central Nebraska's agricultural area. So, we would be remiss if we didn't check out this little watering hole. So, we went there to have a drink and check out this bar located in the middle of the Nebraska prairie.

As the story goes, often told by the bartender, an old timer with a gray beard often wandered into this corn field county saloon, looking for a late afternoon beer and some company. Many patrons said they often saw him here, other folks who were infrequent patrons doubted the story as a false legend. He drove an old faded red 1951 Ford pickup. The old truck had seen a better day on the farm. The after-effects of winter still hung in the overcast air of late April. This old timer was an occasional visitor, but a popular one as related by the bartender.

The Nightcrawlers Bar located In Worms, Nebraska.

No one knew who this old timer was for sure, he was known to travel to the out of the way towns and bars looking for interesting stories and individuals, he seemed to know everyone, but no one had bothered to ask who he was or where he came from. The locals at the bar just called him "Long Beard Hayes". He seemed to know all the stories and history of central Nebraska. Everyone that met him seemed to automatically trust him and accept him as almost someone in the family.

The bartender had captured everyone's attention as he began telling them what happened one cold blustery day in early April. Long Beard Hayes had sauntered into the Nightcrawlers to warm up and have a beer at the bar. He soon was surrounded by several locals; he had that magnetic effect. Each was buying the group at the bar rounds of beer. Hayes had a deep mesmerizing voice and began telling the story of an old single lens spy glass used by the cavalry in the 1860s. The spy glass was found near Worms, Nebraska in a corn field. It was in surprisingly good condition, not scratched, no rust or corrosion yet it looked to have been in the ground for a long time. Why it had not been damaged as the field was plowed and different crops were rotated into it over the years was a mystery. Etched into the barrel was the date 1862.

Looking through the single lens the optics looked as if new, what was viewed seemed to be brighter, more vivid. Some folks who looked through the lens became pale and had frightened looks on their faces and hurriedly put the lens down, others began shaking; a few, who after looking through it, just left the bar in a hurry to never return. Someone asked where the spy glass was now, the bartender said he didn't know. The bartender stopped the story there, that was all he knew. Everyone in the bar was on the edge of their seats, all wanted to know what was next. Suddenly, the door of the bar slowly opened and in walked Long Beard Hayes himself as if on cue. The entire bar fell silent in astonished amazement. No one had seen Long Beard Hayes for several months. Hayes asked for his favorite beer on tap, everyone was staring at him as he sipped his beer. Everyone seemed to know who he was.

When asked about that spy glass he said, "Yes siree "that old scope has seen a thing or two."

How did he know what the conversation was about? He had just come into the bar!

Someone piped in and said, "Where is it now?"

Hayes just looked at him and for a moment and with a slight pause said, "I still have it."

The entire bar was hanging on in anticipation, the TV playing a sports channel seemed to fade into the background.

Hayes went on to say, "One thing about this old Calvary glass, it's an old Civil War relic, buried here after the war by a pioneer on his way out west who was trying to forget the great war between the states."

"He just couldn't handle it, so he buried it because of its eerie power and the horrible memories it seemed to have recorded within its optics."

"After he buried it, it fell into the memories of those who knew it existed."

"A homesteader bought the field where it lay languishing after the war."

Hayes went on to say, "He planted corn there and one night as he walked the field in the cool evening, he saw a light glowing at the exact spot where the scope was laid to rest."

Hayes deep throated voice resonated in the bar as he went on to say, "As the homesteader, his name lost in time, approached the glowing spot in the corn field he saw it protruding out of the soil, so he dug it up!"

At that point in his story a trademark Nebraska thunderstorm hit, and the lights went out. As they flickered back on, Long Beard Hayes was gone. The patrons in the bar rushed out to see if his old red pickup truck was still there, it too was mysteriously gone. Where his truck had been parked, protruding slightly out of the muddy parking lot was an old Confederate States of America belt buckle. Had Long Beard Hayes been that old Civil War pioneer who buried the old scope?

Some, who go regularly to the Nightcrawlers Bar, say Long Beard Hayes is a rebel ghost from the great war between the states, condemned to come back and wander small bars and have unsuspecting thirsty pub dwellers hear the story of the old scope that has seen too much, knows too much of brother killing brother. So, if you venture into a small town in central Nebraska looking for watering hole, be on the lookout for an old red 1951 Ford Pickup driven by an old timer with a long gray beard, he may be carrying an old calvary spy glass.

A Strange Hearing Test

It was time for the annual hearing checkup for Mr. R. Darrol. He was having his ears checked internally closely by the hearing aid specialist and was then instructed to get into the hearing test booth. Both of his hearing aids were removed for the test. The testing booth only has one window looking out over the specialist as the hearing is checked in both ears one at a time using various computerized test equipment. The test booth has one door and is hooked up to a speaker system so the individual being evaluated can hear instructions. The test booth is soundproof with one entry door and is four feet square and eight feet tall. The hearing aid specialist can access the individual being assessed through the door so various hearing test equipment can be used for testing procedures.

R. Darrol was comfortably seated as the door closed for the test. As the door closed the only window suddenly clouded up so Mr. Darrol could not see out and the booth began to tremble and shake. The hearing aid specialist was alarmed, puzzled, and tried to open the door so she could trouble shoot this strange booth malfunction, but the door would not open. Finally, the door just popped open, but she was shocked, Mr. R. Darrol was not seated where he had been just moments before, he was gone!

The specialist began to panic, where was her patient? She double-checked and found that all of the equipment was in working order. She ran out to the waiting room, but he was not there either. The office manager wondered if they were in an earthquake as she felt the building shaking for a moment and said no one had come out of the testing room. Where was Mr. R. Darrol?

The hearing aid specialist rushed back into the testing room as the booth again started shaking and vibrating. The door again popped open and seated back in the booth was Mr. R. Darrol with a 5-day growth of beard. He asked the specialist what was going on with the equipment. He didn't remember much except it suddenly became quite hot and humid. He thought he could hear animal noises and a strange smell filled the booth as if he were in the jungle. As the door popped open, his clothes were sweat soaked as if he had been in a sauna. Inside the testing booth were green vines growing up the insides of the testing booth.

He said suddenly his hearing was extremely sensitive and he could hear noises and talking coming from the waiting room. He also could hear birds outside the window after he left the testing booth. What had happened to him? Where had he gone to have had 5-days of beard growth? The hearing aid specialist said he was gone when the door popped open and that only a few minutes had elapsed until he reappeared. She had only just begun the testing procedure when the booth began to malfunction and vibrate.

Mr. R. Darrol said he felt like he was in a wild undeveloped forest of green with no one around. He had a strange sensation of being somewhere far from his town and the hearing aid testing building. He said he could hear all sorts of animals and jungle sounds before the testing booth door opened. He told the hearing aid specialist he could now hear better than he ever remembered, even when he was a youth. What had happened to him? Where had he disappeared to and why? How was it possible his hearing was now better than normal? To this day the strange hearing aid test and hearing recovery is a mystery to Mr. R. Darrol and is unexplained.

Is Interdimensional Travel a Real Possibility?

Is **Interdimensional Travel a possibility using worm holes?**

Aaron's hyperspace vehicle was now repaired after his narrow escape from a band of space pirates he encountered in a strange alien galaxy. His hyper drive (HD) had become uncontrollable as it took him into a scary and wild dimension he had not selected. He always read his Bible reading scriptures for guidance and protection before his trips into the unknown realms of space travel. This unplanned trip was one of his most frightening. He wanted to return to his appropriate dimension but knew this would be a challenge and prayed for guidance. His hyper drive had suddenly malfunctioned sending him perilously close to time travel. Einsteins Theory of Relativity had been proven correct on my levels of science especially where the processes are time-symmetric and reversible, and the concept of time, according to the second law of thermodynamics, where these processes have a direction and are irreversible.

Perhaps some breakthrough will someday be made for time travel to the future but even if that becomes a possibility, there would be no way to return to the time traveler's proper time. Einstein had indeed unlocked a basic understanding of time as it relates to science. Time travel to the past was indeed impossible, however, the future was another matter in 3001 and science was studying this as a possibility.

Usually, Aaron could select a region of space he wanted to check for signs of life using his HD, his drive was one of the most powerfully designed drives available and it took all of his savings to purchase. He had designed some modifications to the drive making it extremely powerful, so he had to be doubly careful how he dialed-in his trips to not enter what he theorized as time travel. The

Space Federation authorities could easily seize his ship due to his modifications that went against the Orwellian controlled Federation. He could move easily between dimensions; however, extreme caution was needed. This was the year 3001 so travel inter-dimensionally was now a reality and strictly monitored and controlled to stop unauthorized travel to the many unknown and uncharted dimensions that existed on the edge of time. Few intergalactic rocketeers, known in 3001 as Time Jockeys, dared to travel into these uncharted and unknown dimensions and besides that the strict Space Federation regulations prevented all jumps into dimensional travel and was monitored very closely.

Aaron, as a space jockey, was exploring space using power that pushes the limits of time, but he has to be extremely careful. Even though it was 3001, not much was known about time travel and the many unknown problems and unforeseen and unintended consequences caused if time travel even could happen. If speeds were not carefully controlled and monitored Aaron's theory was, he could easily slip into time travel and end up on a baron or deserted planet in a hostile part of the galaxy with no way to return.

Aaron's ship, as did the space pirates ships, needed a special fuel derived from a special fusion procedure.

Aaron also had to constantly be watchful for the notorious space pirates. These brutal space criminals roamed the galaxy looking for hapless planets they could easily rob and pillage. Their small ships could easily enter a planet's outermost atmosphere using a special cloaking power so as to be undetectable. If any detectable riches could be gotten, they would ruthlessly take what they wanted, decimating cultures, and often wrecking the planet with devastating weapons.

Aaron's ship was powered by his own uniquely designed and modified atomic power, using a fusion procedure and hydrogen gas. Atomic fission was available as a backup emergency system so Aaron's ship could return to Earth and not be stranded on a strange alien planet as long as he didn't enter into what he feared would be time travel.

The only good aspect of the Space Federation in 3001 was the federation all but stopping the so-called Sasquatch and Bigfoot sightings from the distant and troubled past history of planet Earth. The unauthorized transportation using worm holes of these monsters from a strange dimension was completely terminated by the strict controls on inter dimensional transportation through space. The space pirates often used these misplaced giant organic anomalies to terrorize a hapless planet in a faraway dimension. Inter spatial dimensional travel was tightly controlled and monitored by the Space Federation and rarely done, like the early astronaut programs in the U.S. However, the wild Space pirates often sent Bigfoot and giant sasquatch type creatures to terrorize a planet before they invaded and confiscated what they wanted.

Aaron was one of the last explorers using interdimensional travel to search the galaxy for interesting species, looking for those planets with the "Goldie Locks" atmosphere supporting life. The only way to find out was by interdimensional travel. Aaron was quite well aware even in his time frame there was no way to get back to his dimension and time if he accidentally went into time travel. Hence the Space Federation had strict control over this type of travel of bending space using wormholes. The very real possibility of travel to the future existed but the extreme expense and technology required was unattainable in 3001 so this type of exploration was not being actively researched. Even in 3001 not much was known or understood about the concept of interdimensional travel and how it affected time.

Aaron knew his hyper drive actually had speeds that could take him into time travel, at least that was his theory. His drive was heavily modified, Aaron was indeed a genius. No technology existed in his time that even approached time travel so his hyper drive was really a breakthrough scientifically, but he wouldn't share it with any space governmental entity for fear of its misuse especially the Orwellian Space Federation.

For the present, Aaron would only dimensionally travel after much careful thought and investigation of a region of space. He did not want to suddenly slip into time travel and be stranded in some strange dimension with no way to return to his time. Aaron's hyper drive used fusion for his main power. Both fusion and fission involve nuclear reactions that release substantial amounts of energy that can be used to produce power. However, fission is the splitting of atoms, while fusion joins them together. Fission spits atoms and has a lot of negative radiation issues, but the fusion Aaron is using joins atoms to generate power without undue radiation. Aaron had to safeguard his uniquely designed hyper drive, he did not want the space pirates to know about his breakthrough invention and modifications and certainly didn't want the space federation to be aware of his design. He clearly was ahead of his time and would take the designs and modifications to his grave if he had to.

He often thought a lot about Nikola Tesla, the futurist electrical engineer born far ahead of his time and his many breakthrough ideas in the 1940s that even in 3001 have not fully understood or adequately interpreted. After his death in 1943 his papers, ideas and all of his possessions were confiscated by the U.S. government just two days after his death in the New Yorker Hotel. Tesla's files and other possessions were sent to Belgrade Serbia where they now reside in the Nikola Tesla Museum. The question has to be asked did the U.S. government return all of his research and documents or is some governmental entity still sitting on some of his research and ideas? An intriguing question.

Aaron had decided to have his research and ideas destroyed should anything happen to him.

The Flying Mogollon Monster of Northern Arizona

Is this a real photograph or not?

The mysterious sightings of the Sasquatch or Big Foot monsters occur all over the U.S. and virtually in every state. However, the largest number of sightings are documented mainly on the west coast and even in Alaska. Arizona has had a fairly large number of Sasquatch sightings over the years that seem to occur in the central part of the state just south of Flagstaff and southeast of Sedona mainly in the Sitgreaves National Forest.

So, one has to wonder when did all of these sightings begin? This phenomenon can be traced back to April of 1890 when supposedly an ape like winged monster with an immense pair of wings was sighted in the desert between the Whetstone and Huachuca Mountains by two ranchers. This beast has also been called the flying Mogollon Monster named after the Mogollon Rim made up of expansive pine tree forests that stretches some 200 miles from Yavapai County in Arizona to the New Mexico state line. All of this was reported in an 1890 issue of the *Tombstone Epitaph* newspaper.

According to the story, these ranchers were armed with Winchester rifles and pursued the beast several miles when they were able to open fire and kill it. According to the reports in the Tombstone newspaper, the creature was exhausted from its long flight from Elizabeth Lake in California and could only fly short distances at a time due to being exhausted. Tombstone had two newspapers at the time, the Tombstone Epitaph, and the Tombstone Nugget.

Apparently in the late 1800s Tombstone was on a steep decline due to sudden flooding of the lucrative silver mines in the area due to an earthquake. Efforts to pump out the water were futile. To improve the economy perhaps this monster story published in the local newspapers could help revive the failing economy with tourism from Tucson, Bisbee and Arizona in general. The town was losing residents who were moving away due to the decline in silver mining.

There is a lot of controversy about a photograph that was supposed to exist of the monster, but no one can seem to find it. Many said they saw it published in the papers, however, in the 1800s not many newspapers were able to publish photographs. The photo above apparently is not the photo in question, and one has to wonder about its authenticity. The Library of Congress has a copy of the newspaper article from the Epitaph issue dated April 26, 1890, on file about the monster and it does not show a photo.

Another sighting near the Grand Canyon of this flying ape-like cryptid was documented in the Arizona Republic newspaper in 1903 and supposedly had two-inch-long claws on talon shaped fingers and was covered in long matted hair and was known to give off blood curdling screams similar to that of a woman's scream but was not aggressive. However, it should also be noted that mountain lions in Arizona also give off screams that sound like a woman. If camping in Arizona be aware of strange flying creatures, you may see the Mogollon Big-Foot like cryptid creature. So, the Arizona flying Mogollon monster legend continues.

References

Aliens, G. A. (n.d.). Retrieved from https://m.imdb.com/title/tt1643266/fullcredits/cast)
and, D. o. (n.d.). Retrieved from https://www.cato.org/blog/deportation-rates-historical-perspective
aol.com/news. (n.d.). Retrieved from https://www.aol.com/news/happens-aliens-pentagon-plan-more-153045730.html

Bob Lazar, former aerospace engineer (discredited, but has a following he also has a criminal record.)

Luis Elizondo (former US Army Counterintelligence).

Some South American countries are open to UAPs and their reporting.

www.ingramcontent.com/pod-product-compliance
Lightning Source LLC
Chambersburg PA
CBHW072210070526
44585CB00015B/1271